REPLICA

REVERBERATIONS OF A SOUL

SUMATHI S

DEDICATION

I solely dedicate these quotes

- To all my supporters, guides and motivators in the Creative Writers Whatsapp group.

- To all my friends, family members and relatives those who are behind my success.

Contents

Contents

Contents

Contents

Disclaimer

The published quotes are the original content of the author. There's no intention of hurting anyone through these quotes. The author assures that the content is 100% plagiarism free.

Acknowledgements

"Acknowledgement is the only way to keep love alive"
Barry Long

Nothing is more important than giving thanks. A simple acknowledgement shows integrity. I would like to pay my special regards to my better half and my daughter for their continuous support.

I'm extremely grateful to Mrs. D. Brinda, Graduate Teacher (English), GHS, Melpattambakkam, Cuddalore dt, who held my hands and showed me the first step in this writing journey.

I would like to express my deepest thanks to Mr. V. Krishnaswami and Mr. A. S. Arunprasath for rendering their support by giving the most valuable foreword.

I would like to extend my deepest gratitude to Mr. G. Thiraviya Kumar, Graduate Teacher (English), GBHSS, Pandanallur, Thanjavur dt and Mrs. P. R. Kalyani, Graduate Teacher (Maths), B.S high school, Athur, Chengalpattu dt for sparing their precious time for editing my quotes.

This project would not have been possible without these people. I never stop thanking them all and I always remember them all in my prayers and in my progress.

Preface

"Books, the unique magical wand
Without any abracadabra
Fills us with knowledge."

This magical book of 150 quotes is a little celebration of words. A fine quote is a valuable gem in the hands of an intelligent and just a pebble in the hands of one who doesn't know its value. This book contains quotes on various topics that will inspire positivity, good and happy feelings. The author tries to give a little inspiration and motivation through her quotes. Whenever anyone needs an extra pep in the steps of the life's beautiful journey, give a pick to this "REPLICA", (Reverberations of a soul), the book of 150 quotes and scroll from the beginning to the end. Embrace everyday of life with these thought provoking quotes.

Foreword

Mr. V. Krishnaswami, B.Com., FCMA.,Consultant - NLC India Limited, Neyveli,Practising Cost Accountant, GST Practitioner,Certified Independent Directior, MHA.

I am very happy to have the occasion to read a book titled "**REPLICA**" which contains thought provoking practical quotations. I am sure this will definitely solace the minds of disturbance when read, at times of turbulence.

Life without hope is- A bird without feathers.

Fly with the wings of hope - To reach your dream woods.

The above quotation is the height of confidence level that a man can imbibe on watching the natural phenomenon. On going through the various aspects compiled in this book of quotes, I am happy to note that enhancing the human value is exhaustively attempted and hence this book will be considered as a good manual in a nice and presentable form.

I congratulate Smt. Sumathi who is receiver of "Kalvi Ratna Award", "Arivu Sudar Gandhi Award", "Kalam Arivu Maamani Award", "Best Teacher 2020 Award",'Woman of Excellence Award", "FCP Excellence Award", "All India Best Writer (AIBA) Award" "Kalvi Sindanaiyalar Award" and certified as one of the "Best Writers", one of the "Consistent Writers" in the Profound Writers group and contributed several others works of this nature.

I am sure that this document would be very useful for all users.

(V. KRISHNASWAMI)

Foreword

Mr. A. S. Arun Prasath,B.Sc(CS);M.A(Eng. Ling);M.Ed.;M.Phil;PGDELT, PGDSE, Ph.D.,GHS, Bathireddihalli, Dharmapuri district.

"You are an open book"

Quote No.: 135

I, ARUN PRASATH A.S, English Graduate teacher from GHS, BATHIREDDIHALLI, DHARMAPURI, feel elated to write this foreword for the fantastic collection of an eminent writer and a friend of mine Mrs. Sumathi. S, a government aided school teacher from SRI KGS HSS, Aduthurai, Tanjore dt.

We are known to each other as lovers of English Language and interested in writing. I have read her previous writing like 'Sparkles of short stories', 'String of pearls', 'Drizzling of Verses' and 'Profound writer's

Anthology'. All of her poems are replicating the life in deeper.

Here is another collection of 185 of her quotes namely 'Replica' which reverberates her soul. On reading the quotes, they just kindled my soul and really felt a complete meditation effect. They were such thoughtful, heart knocking, mind soothing and words of comfort.

I hope all the readers of this book will enjoy reading this book.

I wish my friend with prayers.

(A. S. Arun Prasath)

CHAPTER ONE

HOME PERSONIFIED

Kitchen advised me to eat healthy;
Home theatre insisted me to enjoy music;
Pooja room called me for a prayer to get peace;
Bedroom requested me to sleep at least 6 hours.

LIFE

Falling and rising,
Caring and sharing,
Winning and losing,
Surviving between the
Challenges and Hurdles.

CHAPTER TWO

LOOPING LOVE

Love, an infinite loop, has no end;
It is our life's hope;
No one can avoid to blend.

SOULMATE'S LOVE

My dear soulmate,
I expect my love loop
To start with me and end with you.
Make the loop unbreakable
With your love, care and smile.

CHAPTER THREE

FRAGRANCE OF LOVE

No matter how hard life is,
Never fail to spread
The fragrance of love
With the freshness of a flower.

LIFE WITHOUT HOPE

Life without hope is
A bird without feathers.
Fly with the wings of hope
To reach your dream woods.

CHAPTER FOUR

SMILE

Life is short,
Live it great.
Always keep smiling;
Be the reason behind someone's smile
As peace begins with a smile.

MY VIRTUAL FRIENDS

Nothing to say as secret,
Those who understand me
Remain forever in my heart
As fragrant flowers.
Thanks to all from the bottom of my heart
For recognizing and accepting me.

CHAPTER FIVE

FLAMBOYANT AURA

Everyone has the right to be flamboyant
In their body, heart and spirit;
As they've right to live life in their own way.
Have a lovely sparkle in eyes,
Live life to the fullest.

SHINING AMONG THE STARS

Be a shining star among the super-stars,
With courage and confidence,
With smart work and opulence.

CHAPTER SIX

BE WITH PEOPLE

Be with people who
Encourage our brightness,
Support in our darkness,
Share our pain and sadness,
Fill our soul with gladness.

OPTIMISM

Shine with your own light,
Follow your path in twilight,
Keep on shining, Keep on moving, Keep on smiling.

DEAR INNOCENT

Never try to please anyone,
Be a safeguard for someone.

CHAPTER SEVEN

STRUGGLES

Darkness is necessary
To witness the shining stars.
Struggles in life is mandatory
To chisel us into better ways.

HELP

A kind gesture to reach everyone's heart,
An act of humanity satisfying someone's need,
Supporting the sufferer,
Making someone happier and healthier.

CHAPTER EIGHT

THANKS TO ANIMALS

The large and strong bulls,
The bouvine beautiful cows,
The caprine cute calm goats,
The husky hunky oxen,
Hearty thanks to all...
For being with us
In our tough and tender situations.

ANGER

Basic human emotion that lashes out verbally and/or physically,
Losing patience due to some nuisance,
A strong uncomfortable, non-cooperative response,
An unpleasant feel triggered by an emotional hurt,
Expression of disability when disturbed mentally.
Ponder over the reason for your anger;
You will find it silly.

CHAPTER NINE

LIFE'S A QUIZ

Being a person who is always
Ready to help anyone,
Obviously that puts me
Into a lot of troubles
As no one understands me.
Life is quizzical.

BLOOD DONATION

The best gift of life
To save someone's life
As there's no substitute.

CHAPTER TEN

THE WAIT

Never wait for the perfect moment;
Make every moment perfect;
Infuse life with action;
Live life the best way possible.
Believe in yourself; Pray for betterment.

LAZY AFTERNOONS

Every day is a lazy day;
Every afternoon is crazy.
Make it funny as
Everyone owes an afternoon
That's lazy but you can use it wisely.

CHAPTER ELEVEN

UNIQUENESS

Never think of shinning
One among the stars.
Think of shinning
As the Sun and the Moon,
Showing your uniqueness.

COUNT YOUR BLESSINGS

Whatever I got in my life,
Though they're sometimes a bit too late
Made me completely satisfied;
They're the countless blessings of my life.

CHAPTER TWELVE

DARKNESS

Only in the absence of light
Life may be lit bright
At any time or any moment
Always stay strong.

SANGUINE THOUGHTS

Breathe the fresh air
Add a pinch of positivity
Wash away negativity
Impart sanguine thoughts.

WHAT MY HEART SAYS

Always be simple and silent,
Be loving, caring and working,
Be optimistic and
Be happy with whatever you've.

CHAPTER THIRTEEN

ATTENTION PLEASE

Life is yours
Live it to the fullest
There's no one to save you
Attention please.
Attention is the beginning of devotion
Make your life devoted.

SUNDAY

A day for family time,
Chilling out ourselves is the aim.
The day will clear any way
As the dust settles far away.

CHAPTER FOURTEEN

TELEVISION

Watching television
A nice feast for our vision.
Sometimes it is a piece
That spoils our peace.

LIFE IS LIFELESS

I may be bent but not broken,
I may be scaring but not disfigured,
I may be tired but never lost my hope.
Life is lifeless without hope.

CHAPTER FIFTEEN

CHILD AT HEART

You may be a grown-up;
But, be a child at heart
As long as you can.
Love your inner child
Wonder what will happen at the end.

PERSONIFYING PHONE

My best friend, To share joy and sorrow.
My smartphone danced with me
To the tune of my favourite songs.
My android's alarm wakes me with a pompom.

CHAPTER SIXTEEN

HAPPINESS

Lending a helping hand,
Loving, caring and sharing;
What you think, say and do
All in harmony gives you happiness.

HOPE

Shapes our future, chiseling us into a ruler.
As the light in darkness with
The brightness of success.

COMFORT

A feel of less upset
To give strength, To cheer ourselves.

CHAPTER SEVENTEEN

PLEASE

Avoid backbiting and gossiping; Elude backstabbing,
Don't hurt others' hearts;
Never spoil your soul.

LESSONS FROM NATURE

Be bright as the sun;
Be cool as the moon;
Be strong as the mountain;
Be pleasant as the breeze;
Be adjusting as the river reed.

CHAPTER EIGHTEEN

KNOWLEDGE IS POWER

Knowledge is power;
The entry card to super power;
For a successful future,
To enjoy life's pleasure.

INDEPENDENCE

Full autonomy over life,
Freedom from influence of others,
Ability to move ahead,
For a better and bright future
With confidence and self-esteem.

CHAPTER NINETEEN

HAPPINESS

A feel of fulfillment...
The secret sauce of satisfaction...
The state of tranquility...
The wonderful ornament of life.

PAST

Studying the lessons of yester days,
Learning for the present,
Believing in a better tomorrow.

TIME

The wisest counselor, A sturdy soldier,
The best healer, A wonderful teacher.

CHAPTER TWENTY

MEMORIES

Life may end
But memories have no end card
The valuable treasures of life.

FORGIVENESS

Forgiveness has a scent;
A soothing fragrance
That fills the air with love.

NEGLIGENCE

Live without negligence but
Neglect pain and undesirable from beloved ones.

CHAPTER TWENTY-ONE

NOTHING HURTS

Nothing hurts more than
Being ignored by the ones whom we care,
Being disappointed by the person whom we trust,
Being forgotten by our beloveds.

HAPPINESS IS

Happiness is like a sweet
Taste it;
A flower...smell it;
A nice experience... feel it.

CHAPTER TWENTY-TWO

NOW

Today is our best day;
The present moment is a great gift;
Chisel and shape yourself;
Create your masterpiece now.

NIGHT

Night is a window
To look at the cool moon;
To stare at the shining stars
In the velvet sky.

CHAPTER TWENTY-THREE

MUSIC

Music strikes a chord
At everyone's heart;
Brings tears in eyes;
Soothes the mind and
Consoles the soul.

FOOTWEAR

Best companion...
Ups one's personality
And boosts confidence;
Saves from thorns and weather;
Perfect style of walking.

CHAPTER TWENTY-FOUR

SERENITY

Dear Almighty,
Grant me the serenity
To accept the changes and
To change the things courageously.

DARK NIGHT

After every dark night
There's a bright day.
After every toughest situation
There's the sweetest solution.

CHAPTER TWENTY-FIVE

RAINBOW AMIDST THE STORM

Love and trust are
The rainbows amidst the stormy life.

JUNE

Half of the year gone,
Nothing done,
Fabricate it soon,
Make everything happen in June.

ENDING

There's no real ending
It's just a new beginning.

CHAPTER TWENTY-SIX

COLOURS OF LIFE

Life is a box of crayons
Enjoy the bright colors of positivity
But it won't be complete
Without the darkness of difficulties.

ALONE

Born alone and dying alone,
Why not enjoy being alone
If you wish to be stronger?

CHAPTER TWENTY-SEVEN

SILENCE IS A SIGN

Silence is a sign of strength
As noise creates illusion.
Silence is a sign of wisdom
To avoid many confusions.

SELF RESPECT

An inner quality that
Gives the confidence
To set firm boundaries.

CHAPTER TWENTY-EIGHT

SINGLE

A single candle can both
Defy and define the darkness
A single word can both
Blast or console a heart.

3214 WORDINGS

Unlock your dreams
Unlock happiness
Love
Master key to unlock.

CHAPTER TWENTY-NINE

ESSENCE OF FREEDOM

The struggle for freedom is bitter
But the essence is sweeter.
To taste the sweet essence
Overcome the bitter struggles.

OLD MAN

Don't go for explanations in real life;
Instead, Create Beautiful Moments.
Never be a freak;
Just be unique.

OXYMORON

Ther's a small crowd in front of my house.
There's a deafening silence in the library.

CHAPTER THIRTY

JUSTICE

J - Justness of reason
U - Unfair malice eradication
S - Securing a fair distribution
T - Treating morally without expectation
I - Ideal righteousness
C - Correction of selfish action.
E - Equity.

ENCOURAGE

An act that gives
Support, hope and determination
To feel capable...
To be resilient...
To enjoy life.

CHAPTER THIRTY-ONE

TRUE BEAUTY

Caring and sharing,
Loved and being loved,
In simplicity, beheld
In the eyes of the noble beholder.

DIFFICULT

Ther's nothing more difficult than
Leaving a loving heart,
Holding a hating heart,
Compensating the loss of a lovable heart.

CHAPTER THIRTY-TWO

DON'T FEEL SORRY

If you blindly trusted everyone
Unknowingly they make a fool of you
Or at times use you as curry leaves throwing away as useless.

DON'T BE DISAPPOINTED

When someone's fake face is disclosed,
Or others mistaking you as fake.
Whatever good you do,
It'll always pay you.

SKY

Aim high; Write out new dreams;
Soar up in the sky; But be slow and steady.

CHAPTER THIRTY-THREE

RAINBOW

Colorful sight...
Meeting earth and sky...
Nature's bridge that connects
The earth and the sky.

COVID

Lock yourself at home
Don't try to meet friends or relatives...
Or else they'll block you.

FLIRT

I flirt with writing;
I flirt with art and poetry
As the butterfly with flowers.

CHAPTER THIRTY-FOUR

CONFUSION

Never get confusion;
Learn from past and
You will find a solution.

SATURATION OF THOUGHTS

Human mind is a dramatic;
Saturation of thoughts is quick.
But to follow them is hard and
To achieve is harder.

CHAPTER THIRTY-FIVE

BLOOM

Bloom as a new bud
Spreading the fragrance,
Leave the footprints of love
In the sands of time.

COINCIDENCE

A remarkable concurrence of events
Without apparent connection.
Serendipity is hard to believe
But it agitates the soul
Offers a descry of our destiny.

CHAPTER THIRTY-SIX

LEARNING

Learn from the tough situations;
Make the impossible possible
Envisioning a better future.

LAUGH LIKE

Laugh like the thunder
As it is our stress buster.
Laugh like the lightning
As it reduces our sad feeling.
Laugh like the rain
Laugh with all
As it makes everyone shine.

CHAPTER THIRTY-SEVEN

COMMITMENT

Set goals, Stay committed,
Keep on going ahead, Till you achieve.

LIFE

Life is a race to me;
Never afraid of falling or failing,
Never run with anger or hatred,
Rise and live life with the greatest glory.

HUG

The language of love is to hug
Silent way of expressing warmth...
A special treatment for tranquility.

CHAPTER THIRTY-EIGHT

PROMISE

Better not to promise or never break it.
Either it makes something or destroys everything.

EMANCIPATION

Emancipate yourself from servitude.
Education gives emancipation
Mind can be freed from subjugation
Only by studying your true self.

321 wordings

Care, share, inspire.
Association, affection.
Friendship.

CHAPTER THIRTY-NINE

THE SUN

The sun taught me
To aim high always;
To shine bright with grace;
To make everyone look upright.

FIGHT AGAINST CANCER

Fight against cancer;
Treat it as just a word;
Let faith be stronger
Than the feel of fear.

CHAPTER FORTY

TRANQUIL PLACE

Life commences in a tranquil spot
From the mother's womb.
Life ends in a peaceful site
That's the tomb.

LOVE

Love may be
Either a bless or a curse;
Depends on the person
Whom we love.

CHAPTER FORTY-ONE

NIGHTS ARE MEANT FOR

Nights are meant
For a blissful dream;
To speak with the stars,
To murmur with the moon,
To feel the luxury of sleep,
For a peaceful mind and soul.

LIFE IS A CHAIN

Life is a chain of small sorrows
That ends in great joy.
Life is a chain of memorable moments
That keeps us enthusiastic.
Life is a chain of choices
That changes our life.

CHAPTER FORTY-TWO

DECISIONS

Take problems in a stride,
Accept trial and error.
A wrong decision at the right time is
Better than a right decision at the wrong time.

BEST TEACHER

Time is the best teacher
That teaches great lessons in life.
Never waste it in
Anger, worries, regrets or grudges.

CHAPTER FORTY-THREE

YOUTH

Youth is the solution
To stop corruption.
Build a strong future for the youth
For the future of the nation to be smooth.

INTUITIONS

Intuition is seeing with the soul
Believe in your intuition.
You may be inspired by it
But never follow it
Until you're clear with it.

CHAPTER FORTY-FOUR

LIFE IS A KITE

Life is a kite;
Fly high cautiously in the sky
In the direction of the wind.
Never allow the thread of love
To be cut by someone or something.

IT'S OK DEAR

When we feel worried,
When we're totally drained,
The wonderful words
Calm our mind and heal our heart.

CHAPTER FORTY-FIVE

RAIN

My dear companion,
Entire my life as rain,
Make me blossom and shine,
Add charm to my life chain.

SUCCESS

Success is not a destination;
It's a journey.
Keep on moving
With hope and confidence.

CHAPTER FORTY-SIX

PROBLEMS

Problems we face
In everyday life isn't an end.
It's just the beginning of
A new chapter of life
To make life perfect.

IF DREAMS WERE A BIRD

If dreams were a bird,
It would make us fly
Higher and higher without any boundaries.
Hold fast to the dreams
If dreams die, life will become
A broken-winged bird.

CHAPTER FORTY-SEVEN

PHONE GETS FRUSTRATED

My phone gets frustrated when
Getting unnecessary messages,
Receiving unwanted calls,
Overflowing by forwarded images.

WHEN WE ARE YOUNG

Running happily as deer,
Flying beautifully as butterflies,
Without any duties or responsibilities,
An age of complete happiness.

CHAPTER FORTY-EIGHT

INTENSE THRILL

Life is a thrilling roller coaster
With many ups and downs.
Feel the intense thrill
That makes you chill.

MOUNTAINS

Mountains taught me
How to remain calm
Despite reaching great heights.
How to stand strong
Inspite of many disasters.

CHAPTER FORTY-NINE

GRIEF SHOWS UP

When grief shows up at your door,
Welcome it warmly,
Spend time with it specially,
Gain an experience personally,
To face all unexpected twists of life.

IF LOVE IS A FISH

If love is a fish,
The person who loves is the water,
That makes the fish
To be strong and alive.

CHAPTER FIFTY

IF MY HOME WERE A HUMAN

If my home were a human,
Obviously it would know
All my joys and sorrows,
All my secrets and pains.

WHEN I SAW THE FAIRY

I'll ask the following wishes
To keep me always cheerful,
To make my dreams come true,
To remove discrepancies in the society.

CHAPTER FIFTY-ONE

DECORATION

Decorate life with
Love, kindness and confidence
To make it a celebration.
Live simply, laugh often and love deeply.

LOVE TRIANGLE

Love is a triangle of AUA;
Acceptance, Understanding and Appreciation.
Keep the triangle as a whole
For a lovely lovable life.

CHAPTER FIFTY-TWO

SOCIETY AROUND YOU

Society around is
What you see around you,
How you look into it,
How you take care of it.

THINGS THAT MAKES ME HAPPY

The love of my king,
The smile of my little princess,
The care of my family,
The fruit of my confidence,
The success of my hard work.

CHAPTER FIFTY-THREE

SKY IS THE LIMIT

Sky is the limit
To share our love,
To improve our knowledge,
To prove our talents.

SELFISHNESS

Cease and decay,
Tear off selfishness,
Make life luminous,
Always be generous.

CHAPTER FIFTY-FOUR

HOME TASTES LIKE

Home tastes as a blend of six tastes
Sweet as a chocolate, Sour as a lemonade,
Bitter as a bitter gourd, Pungent as a chilly,
Salty as a popcorn, Astringent as herbs.

WE'RE PASSING DAYS, NOT LIVING THEM

We are just passing days
As we face countless challenges
Physically, mentally and emotionally,
Not leaving us to live our life
With utmost satisfaction.

CHAPTER FIFTY-FIVE

TEAM

T – Together
E – Everyone of us
A – Achieve and get successes
M – More in life.

SINCE THE DAY YOU CAME INTO MY HEART

My mind gets refreshed,
My soul becomes spiritualized,
My body feels energetic
My dear confidence,
Never think of getting out.

CHAPTER FIFTY-SIX

IF WRINKLES COULD SPEAK

If wrinkles could speak,
It would speak about
Not only about the age,
Also about the hard work, pains and sorrows.

WE'RE LIVING IN A WORLD

We're living in a world
Filled fully with ego,
Where people are jealous and greedy,
Where we've to search the oasis of love.

CHAPTER FIFTY-SEVEN

THE NIGHT WELCOMES

The night welcomes
The cool, calm, pleasant moon,
The sparkling shining stars,
To eradicate darkness
Not only in our place
But also in our minds.

EVEN IF YOU DISAPPEAR FROM MY EYES

Even if you disappear from my eyes
Your cute smile, Your bright eyes, Your selfless love,
Always lives with me my dear bubbly baby.

CHAPTER FIFTY-EIGHT

EVERYDAY MY HEART

Everyday my heart
Longs for love,
Yearns for kindness
As the lungs craves for oxygen.

A DAY WITHOUT A FRIEND

A day without a friend is
A day without brightness.
A day without happiness is
A day without moral support.

CHAPTER FIFTY-NINE

GRIEF DISAPPEARS WHEN

Grief disappears when
I lean on my consort's shoulder,
I gaze at my little princess's smile,
I reach my destination successfully.

YOU'RE AN OPEN BOOK

My dear friend,
You're an open book
To learn many things,
To guide me in the right path.

CHAPTER SIXTY

THE SECRET TO LIVE A LONG LIFE

The secret to live a long life is
Leaving the footprints of love
Wherever you go,
Whatever you do.

MY FIRST ONLINE FRIEND

My first and foremost online friend,
A friend forever
Who soothes my soul is
Music and music only.

CHAPTER SIXTY-ONE

WRITING A BOOK

Writing a book is to
Make us eternal
With our words
Through our thoughts.

DARKNESS IS A TUNNEL

Darkness is a tunnel
Everyone has to pass through.
Cross it with courage
To reach the destination.
Without passing darkness
There's no happiness.

CHAPTER SIXTY-TWO

ONLY A WRITER KNOWS

Only a writer knows
How to hide pains,
How to express emotions,
How to share happiness.

WAITING

Waiting is a
Sign of love,
Sign of hope,
Sign of patience.

CHAPTER SIXTY-THREE

TO WAKE UP FRESH

To wake up fresh
Everyone needs a peaceful slumber
Free from illusions,
Free from unwanted dreams.

AS I GET OLDER

As I get older,
Salt and pepper in my hair,
May be some wrinkles in skin.
Changes will be only physically
Always sweet sixteen mentally.

CHAPTER SIXTY-FOUR

I WISH I COULD HOLD YOU

My dear family,
I wish I could hold you like
The root of a plant,
The power of a battery,
The heartbeat of a human.

THE BEST FRIEND OF MORNING

A gentle breeze
With the fragrance of fresh flowers,
A cup of hot coffee,
The lovely smile of our loved ones.

CHAPTER SIXTY-FIVE

MY HEART SKIPS A BEAT

My heart skips a beat when
I hear of child abuse, when
I witness society's inequality, when
I know about the problems of unemployment.

THE LONGEST NIGHTS ARE

The longest nights are
The lonely nights,
Longing for a shoulder to lean
To beat out stress and anxiety.

CHAPTER SIXTY-SIX

CONFIDENCE – PRESENCE & ABSENCE

Your absence reminds me
The importance of your presence.
Your presence teaches me
To grasp the reality of life.

THE STREET IS QUIET

The street is quiet at night;
But it has many mysteries,
Hidden many histories,
Remain silent with secrets,
Dwell as a witness
For many unrevealed love stories.

CHAPTER SIXTY-SEVEN

LIFE IS A SERIES

Life is a series of challenges
Never feel downtrodden.
Have courage and confidence
To confront even the toughest situation.

THE FUTURE BELONGS TO

The future belongs to
Only those who work hard.
Never try to predict it
Instead create it.

CHAPTER SIXTY-EIGHT

SLEEP IS MY BEST FRIEND

Sleep is my best friend
With whom I can
Dream my dreams,
Heal my pains,
Revitalize for a new beginning.

OUTSIDE MY HOME

A wonderful world is waiting,
To strengthen my thoughts,
To build my bravery,
To make me a successful person.

CHAPTER SIXTY-NINE

TRUE LOVE

An ever growing process, Never ending trust,
The honey of life, A long lasting emotion,
The greatest power of existence.

NAMESTRY - MY FAVOURITE PERSON

D – Dazzling beauty
A - Affectionate
U - Unique
G – Genuine, generous
H – Handsome, harmonious
T – Tender hearted
E - Elegant
R – Radiant personality

CHAPTER SEVENTY

GIFT

A symbol of love, A sign of gratitude,
Strengthen the bond with family and friends.

RESPECT

R - Reliable
E - Earnest
S – Spirited highly
P - Philanthropic
E - Empathetic
C - Captivating
T – Tangible

CHAPTER SEVENTY-ONE

LOVE

L – Land of happiness
O – Ocean of cheerfulness
V – Valley of pleasure
E – Energiser of life.

MOTHER'S WOMB

The safest place, The purest place, The closest place,
Where life commences.
The place of humanity
Where a child grows with sincerity,
Without knowing the world's reality
As a symbol of purity.

CHAPTER SEVENTY-TWO

ENJOYMENT

Living in peace and harmony
With our body, mind and soul,
An incredible energizer for human life.

SEE SAW

Life is a see saw
Be ready to pair with someone,
Shows the ups and downs of life,
Stay balanced and aim high.

CHAPTER SEVENTY-THREE

GIVE HIM NOT A FISH, TEACH HIM TO FISH

Stand for something, To get anything.
Keep smiling, Life is a beautiful thing.
Build the guts enough
To face whatever the consequences.
Learn yourself to fish
To satisfy your wish.

PATIENCE

Capacity of tolerance,
Bearing of provocation and irritation,
Maintaining good attitude in everything,
Ability to handle children and aged one.

CHAPTER SEVENTY-FOUR

DEDICATION

Believe in yourself,
Have pride and dedication,
Be devoted to the idea,
Brings us the fruit of success.

PRAYER

Confidence in the power of the Almighty,
Words of affirmation and wisdom,
A devout petition to God,
The best medicine for all problems.

CHAPTER SEVENTY-FIVE

COOL DRINKS

It's so hot outside,
A burning sense inside,
Chill yourself with a cup of cool drinks.
Chill, chill; cool, cool;
Feel as if you're in a pool.

HEALTH

The foundation for a happy life,
A precious asset,
A complete physical, mental, social well-being,
The complete harmony of the body, mind and spirit,
The greatest gift, the greatest wealth.

CHAPTER SEVENTY-SIX

A NEW START

A new fresh start
May be simple or hard,
May be tough or tender,
Just let it go
To learn something new
To reach the destination
To beget the fruit of success.

LIFE IS

Life is a ship in the sea,
Be the captain with a glee
To complete the journey of life
In between the rough and coarse waves.

CHAPTER SEVENTY-SEVEN

MOTHER'S LOVE

A protective possessive affection,
Lies in the heart of every child
An unconditional and never ending love.
FATHER'S LOVE
Full of hidden sacrifices,
Kind, selfless, faithful and humble love,
The anchor of his child's life.

CHAPTER SEVENTY-EIGHT

BELIEVE IN YOURSELF

Just be yourself,
Believe you can.
Be strong in your belief,
Be brave in your pursue,
Be smart in whatever you do,
No one can beat you.

PEACE OF MIND

Life with inner peace without stress.
Liberty in tranquility
Faith in god's ability.
Being loyal, calm and happy
Out of greed, jealous and enmity.

CHAPTER SEVENTY-NINE

LIFE (LIMERICK)

Life is a beautiful thing
Lead it as a king,
Always with a smile
Attract everyone with your life style
Until you achieve everything.
Whatever the situation,
Do everything with dedication.
Life is finding ourselves and creating ourselves,
Always be an inspiration.

FREEBIES

If we get freebies,
We are mortgaging our freedom,
Either we've stuff or not
Keep your head up, Keep your heart strong,
Be great to avoid freebies.

CHAPTER EIGHTY

I'M CURIOUS

As a teacher, I'm curious to know
The results of my students,
As it gives me cent percent satisfaction.
As a mother, I'm curious
To know about my ward's future
That makes me happy and cheerful.
As a human, I'm always curious
To keep on moving forward,
To open new doors, To do good and new things.

HAPPY GANESH CHATHURTHI

Let Lord Ganesha bags us
Happiness as big as his appetite,
Life as long as is trunk,
Pains and troubles as his mouse,
Memorable moments as sweet as his laddu.

CHAPTER EIGHTY-ONE

IT'S BEEN A YEAR ALREADY

It's been a year already
Not a year only, more than a year,
Locked in home due to the pandemic.
It's all in our hands
Either to be locked again or to be freed.

YOUR EYES MADE ME

Your eyes made me mad
But the madness
Brings me happiness.

CHAPTER EIGHTY-TWO

IF NIGHT WERE A PERSON

If night were a person,
It would fill my loneliness
Holding it tightly
I'll lead my life bravely.

LIFE IS A QUESTION

Life is a question paper
Never think it tougher,
Find the solution that's easier.
If you solve a question
Life will give you another.

CHAPTER EIGHTY-THREE

MY MOTHER

A walking miracle,
A priceless jewel.
A multi-tasking persona,
Shining in life's arena.

TSUNAMI

T - Tidal waves...
S - Sudden strong surging
U - Unexpected
N - Nightmarish
A - Angry
M - Mysterious
I - Infuriating waves

CHAPTER EIGHTY-FOUR

SAVE THE EARTH

Let us go green
To make our globe clean.
Save the earth
At least selfishly
For, our wellbeing solely
Depends on its mirth...

EDUCATION

A passport for future,
A password for freedom,
A key to unlock the world,
A movement from dark to bright.

CHAPTER EIGHTY-FIVE

A DECADENT SLICE

Life is what you bake,
Bake it as sweet as a honey cake,
With the secret ingredient of sincere love.

MIRTH

M - Mind often thinks of
I - Irresponsible, irrelevant thoughts
R - Rarely being happy
T - Take your concerns from the worldly affairs
H - Happiness is at your doorsteps.

CHAPTER EIGHTY-SIX

LIFE IS A CHAIN

Life is a chain of small sorrows
That ends in great joy.
Life is a chain of memorable moments
That keeps us enthusiastic.
Life is a chain of choices
That changes our life.

TAJMAHAL

T – Typical, tantalizing
A – Amazing, angelic
J – Jimp, jocund
M – Magnetic, majestic
A – Adorable, admirable
H – Holy, hunk
A - Aglow
L – Lively, lovely

CHAPTER EIGHTY-SEVEN

EMOTIONS

The universal language,
The authentic expression,
The unique part of human experience.
Emotions make a human
Never play with it as an insane.
Be the master of thoughts,
Never be the slaves of emotions.

POETRY IS

Poetry is an art of imitation,
Filled with our emotion.
Poetry is the extra ordinary language
Every human life's patronage.

CHAPTER EIGHTY-EIGHT

SIBLINGS

Brother and sister together
Ready to face whatever
What life gives them in future
In a wonderful shelter.

LONG LASTING LOVE

Love kindles life,
Long lasting love shapes life,
Makes everything beauty
In our life journey.

CHAPTER EIGHTY-NINE

EXAM WISHES

Marks alone never decide one's destiny,
Live in the present, give your best,
Be dedicated in your efforts,
without watching the clock.
Study with right friends
Convert your efforts into victories,
Without spoiling the health.
May an ocean of good luck and success
Falls through out exams and in life too.

CHAPTER NINETY

EMOTIONAL REJUVENATION

Forget and forgive,
Burst out your tears,
Wash away sadness,
Rejuvenate,
Wipe out the negativity,
Establish yourself in positivity.

ABOUT THE AUTHOR

Mrs. S. SUMATHI, M.A., B.Ed.,SRI KGS HSS, ADUTHURAI,THIRUVIDAIMARUDUR TK, THANJAVUR DT.

Mrs.S.Sumathi, has the degree of M.A(English) & B.Ed. She has been working in Sri KGS HSS, Aduthurai, Thiruvidaimarudur TK, Thanjavur Dt, a Govt aided school. Her goal is to get Dr.Radhakrishnan's "The Best Teacher" Award. She is a budding short story Writer. One of her short stories was published in "Sparkles of Short Stories" and "Spitfire Soul." She has written more than 500 poems on various topics. Her first 100 string of poems were published by December 2020 in the name of “String of Pearls.” Her second book of 100 poems "Drizzling of Verses" was published by October 2021. Apart from this, she has been a co-author in “Rainbow of Verses”, “Mesmerizing Honey Drops”, “Profound Writers Anthology”, “Echoes” “Glitters of Creative Writers" and "Forbidden clouds." One of her poems was published in "The beauty of creation and love", a World Book of Records in which 1111 poems were there written by 1111 poets. Her articles and poems were published in Namaste India, an E-magazine. She is a receiver of “Kalvi Ratna Award”,”Arivu Sudar Gandhi Award”, ”Kalam Arivu Maamani Award”, “Best Teacher 2020 Award”, “Woman of Excellence Award”, “FCP Excellence Award”, “All India Best Writer (AIBA) Award” "Kalvi Sindanaiyalar Award" and certified as one of the “Best Writers”, one of the “Consistent Writers” in the Profound Writers group. Always she wishes to be the best teacher and the best human.

9 798886 849073

Printed by Libri Plureos GmbH in Hamburg,
Germany